RECALIBRATE

A STRATEGIC GUIDE
FOR ACCELERATED GROWTH

SUSAN SPAULDING

DEDICATION

To my husband, George,
for his unconditional support
of my business pursuits.

CONTENTS

Acknowledgments

About Recalibrate Strategies and Susan Spaulding

ACKNOWLEDGEMENTS

Although many colleagues and business partners have been important to my understanding of business strategy, I want to offer particular thanks to the twenty executives (listed below) that you'll meet in this book. Their insights and experiences brought the Recalibrate concepts to life.

Special thanks to:

Mary Bentley, Marketing Executive, Food Industry
Bill Bernardo, APC, Inc.
Pam Berneking, Alterra Bank
Claire Brand, Hallmark Cards, Inc.
Jeffrey Byrne, Jeffrey D. Byrne + Associates
Harry Campbell, Durrie Vision
Gina Danner, NextPage
Fred Embry, Power Group Companies
Gordon Harton, GFH Business Consulting, LLC
Joyce Hayhow, Kansas City Business Journal
Rich Mathews, Newell Rubbermaid
Sam Meers, Meers Advertising, Inc.
Maria Meyers, U.S. SourceLink & KCSourceLink
Dr. Michelle Robin, Your Wellness Connection, P.A.
Teri Rogers, Hint
Keith Pigues, Executive, Professor, Author and Speaker
Sandy Smith, AmSurg Corp.
Gary and Trish Walker, Magic Touch Cleaning, Inc.
John Wendler, Tractor Supply Co.
Lavon Winkler, Milbank Manufacturing Company

CHAPTER ONE

IF YOU'RE HEADED FOR THE STARS, CALIBRATING ONCE WON'T DO

For nine months, the Mars Climate Orbiter was speeding through space and communicating with NASA using metric measures in its reporting. But the engineers on the ground were replying using the non-metric English system. The mathematical mismatch was not caught until after the $125 million aircraft was sent crashing too low and too fast into the Martian atmosphere.

Lack of recalibration meant dramatically missing the mark.

During the Falkland Islands War, the British destroyer HMS Sheffield was sunk by a direct missile hit to the ship. The ship's radar warning systems were programmed to identify the destructive Exocet missile as "friendly" because the British arsenal includes the Exocet's homing device, so the destroyer's warning system saw it as no threat.

Lack of recalibration produced disaster.

For two full days back in 1991, telephone service was disrupted in Washington DC, Pittsburgh, Los Angeles and San Francisco; twelve million people were affected. The crash came because of a single mistyped character in one line of code in the software-managed telephone switching stations.

Failing to recalibrate even a little at a critical time can cost customers and trust.

Not just calibrating, once-and-done, but recalibration matters. It matters in space exploration, and war, and large-scale communications, and it matters in your business.

Recalibrating is a mindset. It means knowing when hard right turns are necessary. It means encouraging disruption and creating a culture where you examine what was and what is, then readjust for what can be.

What can recalibration do for you?

In today's competitive marketplace, companies are looking for paths to create short-term solutions and longer-term opportunities that will accelerate their business and brand growth. You may lead one of those companies.

Recalibration can help you find that path. The four tenets of Recalibration – Relevance, Differentiation, Engagement and Expression – can become the signposts that take you to new success. Learning to recalibrate will show you:

- How to harness the knowledge that already exists within your organization
- How to break down barriers to change and introduce disruption and creative problem solving
- How to know what measurements matter
- How to find your red flags and how to turn red flags to opportunities

Once you can recalibrate your current business approach, it will help you to find new ways to market your company. Even with old products, you can rebrand and present them in new and fresh ways. In a sense, even old products can become the basis for new product ideas.

Of the companies on the Fortune 500 list in 1955, more than 80% are no longer what they were. Those companies either went bankrupt, merged, or fell off the list.

This happened to some because they simply lost focus.

Where is your focus? Do you know? Here are five questions that can help you evaluate.

- Do you have a reasonable number of objectives?
- Are the objectives clear?
- Do you have the resources to achieve your objectives?
- Do your employees know what to do and are they believers in your mission and methods?
- Are you tracking your progress?

If you said yes to all of the above, you may not need to re-calibrate. But if you said no to any, it is likely time to take stock and re-focus on what matters most.

The components of recalibration

In the pages ahead, you'll find the stories of many who have successfully recalibrated some aspect of their business.

Here you'll see in action the four integral components that have made the difference in these companies' successes and can make a difference in yours.

Relevance means knowing what matters, matching organizational competencies and goals to current and emerging consumer interests.

Differentiation points to brands that matter, building products and positioning that create a clear and unique sense of value.

Engagement comes from the connections that matter. It happens when you create brand ambassadors of employees, consumers and all those in the value chain by including them in creating and delivering on what you do.

Expression means the stories that matter. It means finding and delivering the essence of a clear and compelling story to maintain engagement.

Recalibration and you

So, what difference can recalibration make to you? Years of working with clients have convinced me that recalibrating can change your effectiveness with your customers, your brand, and your organization. Here's what I mean.

With customers,

- You can earn a greater share of your current customers' total spending
- You can attract new customers
- You can create a customer experience that sets you apart from all others
- You can discover new market opportunities

With your brand,

- You can breathe new life into an existing brand
- You can increase new product success
- You can become iconic to the category
- You can create a strong community and more rapidly build trust

With your organization,

- You can improve the value of your company
- You can more effectively deploy resources
- You can be recognized as a great place to work
- You can create a culture of innovation

From the Mars missions to your mission

Maybe you're not trying to land a spacecraft on Mars, but you are trying to land that next customer.

Maybe you're not tasked with protecting a Navy destroyer from missile attack, but you are trying to protect your brand from being lost in an ocean of sameness.

And maybe you're not trusted with keeping telecom communications functional in four major cities at once, but you are trusted with keeping your employees aligned to your purpose in ways that make for a great customer experience.

Recalibration would have made a difference in the success of each of these challenges; it can make a difference for you.

CHAPTER TWO

RELEVANCE: KNOWING
WHAT MATTERS

Matching organizational competencies and goals

to current and emerging consumer interests

Relevance is about knowing what matters, both to you and to those in the marketplace you intend to reach.

And relevance requires connectivity. It means the coming together of what matters to your company with what matters to your customers.

Remember back when Xerox was lauded for having the strongest sales organization of most any company? A magnificent accomplishment. Problem was, in that focus on selling excellence, they neglected to look carefully at the future of what they were selling, from their customers' viewpoint. While they cranked out better copier sales numbers than other copier manufacturers, customers were moving their production preferences to their computer printers.

Or consider the Boeing Sonic Cruiser. In 2001, Boeing claimed it would revolutionize air travel by providing a large jet that could fly at just under the speed of sound, 20% faster than today's commercial jets.

But a year into development, Boeing discovered to its chagrin that the airlines for which it was designing didn't want more speed. The airlines sought cheaper planes with high operational capacity.

Oops.

What's the point of being the best if what you're best at is...irrelevant?

What is relevance?

Relevance isn't a static state; it's dynamic.

Think Kodak. Who would have imagined just a few years back that the company who gave us "Kodak Moments" would in 2012 be declaring bankruptcy?

Sure, the company can be credited with transforming photography from a domain dominated by formal-portrait professionals to a hugely popular one that became essential to our daily lives. But when a camera company stays riveted to its flagship product rather than landscape-aware as the world moves to digital photography, failure is inevitable. Kodak tried to ignore new technology hoping it would go away by itself, leaving intact its iconic brand and current highly-lucrative revenue streams (film sales had gross margins of 70%). And strategy was cemented in Kodak's then successful business model, not users' shifting needs.

That's a no-fail formula for obsolescence.

Why relevance matters

It reduces risk of failure.

You face decisions about content and messaging strategy, innovation strategy, product portfolio strategy, and more. And with each of these decisions comes inherent risk of failure. But when you are assured of your product's relevance, you know whom you are reaching, and how to present the facts and features to attract them. Relevance can be a failure-mitigator.

It leads to smarter marketing choices.

Remember John Wanamaker's not-so-tongue-in-cheek observation: "Half the money I spend on advertising is wasted; the trouble is, I don't know which half." When our products and services make sense to customers, and scratch where they itch, the investments we make promoting them produce healthier returns. We waste our dollars when we do a great job touting irrelevant products.

It makes for genuine partnerships that serve both marketer and customer.

An ingredient company I worked with saw sales increase as they began to customize their products, adding SKU's specific to just one or two customers but without charging extra for this service. Not surprisingly, as their product portfolio ballooned, profits shrank.

Was the increased customization relevant to customers? The sales figures assured them it was. Problem was, the customization strategy wasn't relevant to the company. Indeed, had it continued, it might have run them right out of business.

As it turned out, in talking with customers, an increased level of customization had been undervalued; customers were willing to pay a premium to get it. But relevance had to hold true for both partners in the supply/demand equation to have power.

Relevance requires continual tending

I've seen scenarios that seem to be relevance-killers, if they aren't tended to carefully.

When companies try to be all things to all people.

A restaurant chain I worked with had been first in their category for some time, resulting in a strong following. But over time, their understanding of the power of their uniqueness blurred, and strategy began to drift them toward casual dining, a much broader competitive category. What looked like an intuitive move toward greater market share actually diluted both their leadership position and the clearly differentiated reason for customers to continue to choose them. What looked like an expansion strategy actually produced contraction in guest visits and profits.

When acquisitions don't align with a company's core competencies.

A company that produced insulated coolers sought a product line that would offset the seasonal nature of cooler sales. Though a good strategy, their choice was convection heaters, and the result was a definite "cooling" in profitability. Because they had no fundamental understanding of the category, including the sales channel, relevance declined, taking profits with it.

When companies guess the demand for a product without validating the potential opportunity.

This one happens often in looking at adjacent markets for growth opportunities. Customers are clamoring for your primary offering; doesn't it make sense they'd also demonstrate the same demand for something that complements it, or makes it more effective, or differently useful? Maybe, maybe not. Without evaluating the adjunct product with as much rigor as you did your flagship product, relevance may suffer.

When companies aren't ready to move with rapid market shifts.

Innovative technology can make yesterday's hot product obsolete. New focus on a social issue like sustainability can undermine credibility of products once thought reasonable.

Relevance can't be taken for granted; it is as static as your teenage daughter's latest crush.

But we believe we are relevant...

Really? Check yourself for these five warning signs of looming irrelevance.

1. You are continuing to grow revenues, but this growth is either market-influenced or acquisition-driven, rather than year-over-year growth from core products.
2. You are delivering necessary profits, but no reinvestment is going on in the business.
3. You have high customer satisfaction, but your customer base is shrinking.
4. You have strong brand awareness, but you aren't delivering on what you've promised.
5. You are getting new customers, but there are high levels of churn.

If any of the above is true for you, you may be moving into the Relevance Danger Zone.

So, before you slide down a slippery slope to irrelevance, here are the diagnostics I call on to determine whether or not a relevance check is in order.

- Is profitability declining?
- Am I adding new customers?
- Am I increasing share of wallet with current customers?
- Do my customers believe I am delivering on what is promised?
- Am I losing to a competitor (Market share? Shelf space?)

And, second in importance, but still good diagnostics:

- Is my product lifecycle waning?
- Is there a higher churn rate?
- Is customer satisfaction declining?
- Are customer visits declining?

How do you stack up against these nine diagnostics for relevance?

Increasing relevance

Your strategy becomes more relevant to your customers when you include your value chain (suppliers, sellers, consumers and influencers) in the creation of your products.

How to get there? Three must-haves will make your efforts productive:

First, a big dose of introspection is required, along with a culture open to hard right turns.

Second, a continuous flow of information about key indicators that might suggest change is required. Consider your financial condition, the market, the competition, the distribution channels and the consumers.

Third, knowledge from many different sources is required, so decisions to change are based on validated insights.

Then, careful, purposeful steps forward will lead you to a design for relevance that is both timely and flexible.

1. Create a more tightly focused characterization of the target consumer.
2. Create a complete understanding of how your product moves through the value chain.
3. Track sales activity at an individual customer level to define your best customer and lifecycle position.
4. Track sales by SKU, product grouping or brand to identify the product lifecycle position.
5. Agree to decision criteria that keep your organization focused on core competencies, goals and strategies.
6. Narrow your focus to a short list of strategic imperatives rather than a long task list.

With these six steps as your guide, you'll find relevance becoming less ambiguous, more definable and actionable.

Relevance sticking points

Companies I've worked with over time have found that certain points in the relevance-recalibration process come harder than others. And some respond better to warnings as they develop strategy than they do to positive steps. So, in response, I've identified these "sticking points" for a strong, flexible relevance strategy.

You risk irrelevance if...you make strategy decisions solely on anecdotal evidence coming from the field.

You risk irrelevance if...you rely solely on financial metrics, disregarding external influencing factors.

You risk irrelevance if...you don't pay attention to new competitor entrants or changing competitor strategies.

You risk irrelevance if...you aren't connecting with your customer's changing needs and wants.

You risk irrelevance if...you think you know better than your customer.

You risk irrelevance if...you aren't sharing the vision and engaging your entire organization in the goals and strategies and how they are changing with the times.

A final caution

To maintain relevance, timing is everything.

Changing economics, changes in competition, changes in value perceptions can put a company or even an industry on a downward spiral very quickly. The market research industry, for example, forfeited its value position with the C-suite to management consulting firms. I felt a personal investment in this change because much of my career has been tied to the market research industry.

The industry chose to focus on its data gathering and providing objective information rather than on the business impact this information could have. As a result, the industry was pushed to the side and it has been struggling to find its way back to relevance ever since.

Moving slowly can be the kiss of death.

As you refocus on relevance, you'll have put in place the first and most critical building block for a winning strategy.

Leaders on Relevance

Gina Danner, CEO NextPage

We think it's important to get as close to the end purchaser as we possibly can. Our job is to make our clients money; that's the only job we have.

Teri Rogers, CEO Hint

Our business landscape has changed dramatically. Previous focuses on television commercials for ad agencies, and on corporate communications have been ripped apart by shifts in the economy and changes in technology. Our core competencies as a production company remain the same. But now we stand for the fusion of design, technology and innovation. That's what makes us relevant.

Gordon Harton, GFH Business Consulting, LLC

My point of view in product management is anchored in understanding what need the product satisfies. If you can deliver on that, you can succeed. But there's no need to recalibrate to reach a new market if the brand does not and will not resonate with that market.

I believe 80% of the solution is identifying the problem. We can solve almost anything if we know the real problem. Most people look at solutions before they know the cause, and wind up creating excellent answers to an irrelevant question.

Harry Campbell, CEO Durrie Vision

If you tell me your strategy is to generate profit or revenue, I laugh. That's not a strategy – it's everyone's goal. So, in looking at relevance, I ask, "What do you say 'no' to?" A product-based company may need to say no to auxiliary products that could be generated from their primary product. Or maybe it's no to certain distribution channels. It isn't that these might not make money, but strategically if you are trying to move too many things down the field a little bit at a time, you'll never be wildly successful at anything.

SVP, Industrial Materials Company

After initial success as a company, we began to lose relevance by staying focused on the domestic marketplace while missing shifts toward a global marketplace. In time, we eventually went into bankruptcy, and then reorganized.

One of the greatest revelations of that period was this: because we had been the market leader, our demise scared the customer base. For the first time in our history, we realized the importance we had to our customers. So when we recognized that, we came out with a new direction. We cleansed ourselves of some industry practices that inhibited our performance, and focused practices and products on the customers who saw us as critical to their success.

CHAPTER THREE

RECALIBRATING FOR

RELEVANCE

LAVON WINKLER

MILBANK MANUFACTURING COMPANY

Milbank builds solutions that move power for the residential, commercial, industrial, utility and transportation sectors. Milbank combines more than 80 years of expertise in electrical distribution with a commitment to develop and globally implement sustainable, integrated power solutions. Milbank's portfolio includes electric metering systems, wind and solar solutions, electrical vehicle charging stations and portable power. A third-generation, family-owned business, Milbank Manufacturing Company is headquartered in Kansas City, Mo. with an employee base of over 500. Currently Milbank manufacturers over 19,000 items which include: metering devices, industrial enclosures and controls, such as junction boxes, telephone cabinet covers, transformer cabinets, and more. Next-stage development includes generators, transfer switches and energy management solutions.

When Lavon Winkler came to Milbank about eight years ago, the company positioning in the market told a misleading story. Milbank had been profitable, growing year over year with 45% of market share. However, a deeper look showed it was actually under siege. The housing industry, which Milbank served, was growing faster than in the past. Winkler observed, "When you're growing at a lesser rate than the market, you are actually losing market share."

The intuitive solution seemed to be innovation, to start pushing out new products and grow yourself back to relevance.

But Winkler knew real relevance had to start with Milbank's core competencies in production. It was this core, Winkler decided, that first needed to be strengthened in order to earn the right to innovate.

Strengthening the core

A solid core meant changes in production. Though the company was profitable, operating metrics didn't reflect that success. Milbank owed long-term debt; lead times on some products were 26 weeks; shipments went out on-time 60% of the time.

So, initiatives focused on moving Milbank to lean manufacturing to increase efficiencies and reduce its manufacturing footprint while increasing production capacity.

The company also took a deeper look at its customers. The core business in the United States involved anyone selling electricity to end users, such as the utility companies, the rural electric cooperatives, the municipalities, and more. Adding all those up, Milbank found about 3,000 potential entities in the U.S. needed their product.

But each wanted its own version of the meter socket, and individualized variations on its version.

Winkler observed, "You can either look at that situation and lament, or ask how we can use it to our strategic advantage. It looked to us like most wouldn't want to enter our niche, because the barrier to entry is having to produce a large number of SKUs and do them very well. So, we decided to continue to grow in our niche by answering that need."

Having so many SKUs would mean very small run sizes, but with a lean model done very well, 170 model changes during a shift became the norm.

Investing in the core makes for resilience and growth potential

With refocused production and greater efficiencies, the company was able to retire all its debt in 2007. So, during the Great Recession, Milbank was able to adjust quickly, and when others shrank back in fear, the company was able to continue to build so when the market turned around it would be ready to capitalize on it.

When the turn came, Milbank moved its market share from 45% to 60%, and began a self-funded venture into technology. A solid base gave Winkler the right to ask questions about innovation.

"When I looked ahead," Winkler said, "I wanted headlines about us to talk not about Milbank, the socket company, but Milbank, the technology company. But what should that look like? What might a fit be for us?"

He began to investigate by assigning his Vice-President of Research and Development to look at renewable energy and the thinking behind the smart grid. That investigation led to a conviction to build intelligence into the devices Milbank was known for, then growing from there. So they partnered with a company in Cambridge, England, to begin developing ideas.

Studying renewable energy led the company into developing point-of-use interfaces that connected energy generated from renewable sources like wind and solar, to end users.

Connecting the strong and expanding core to customer needs

Once Milbank could begin innovation from a position of focused strength, customers took notice.

Winkler observed, "Our top five customers are significant purchasers of our products; but they are also very large companies. Let's say we sell them $7 million dollars worth of products that might be a big book of business for us. But many of these are $5-7 billion dollar entities. So if you take seven million as a percentage of seven billion, we were not major players with them.

"However, remember that we decided to be uniquely valuable by being the only ones that provide national coverage for thousands of SKUs, so we mattered to our customers.

"As an example, when we were trying to get an entry point into the generator business, we wanted to join with Briggs & Stratton because of their quality and name recognition. But once we agreed to join forces, Briggs asked that we lead with the Milbank name instead of theirs. In our channel, the Milbank brand was stronger than Briggs & Stratton. Distributors knew we wouldn't bring them junk."

So, once Milbank began to venture into renewable energy, and then generators, the companies they worked with took notice.

Winkler continued, "I knew something big had happened the day I sat across the table from one of our big-name customers, and he started the meeting by saying, 'I want to know: what woke up Milbank? You've been a meter socket company forever; now you've got this, you've got that. How did this happen?' As a result of this attention, we found these large customers began to say, 'How are we going to grow this business?' instead of 'How are you going to help me grow my business?'"

Listen and Learn = Relevance

Now Milbank measures success as much by learning from customer interactions as by sales. They look to the future to try to see a need the customer has yet to recognize.

"We go and have conversations, " Winkler says. "We listen and observe. Then we come back and review what we heard for opportunities; not short-term, in-and-out opportunities, but ones that will make a difference in the long-term."

When you strengthen and focus your core,
you can come to customers
with a clear sense of what you do well.
From this positioning, a willingness to listen
to customers' needs can provide new value
that translates to ongoing growth.

CHAPTER FOUR

DIFFERENTIATION: BRANDS THAT MATTER

Building products and positioning that create

a clear and unique sense of value

If awards were given for branding sameness, the top five winners would all be weight loss clinics. I wonder sometimes if there's an online template for their advertisements because they all feature the same two themes: "before" obese girl, then "after" in a sassy bikini, and the obligatory "huge jeans/tiny jeans" shots.

Contrast this to the perspective of banking CEO Pam Berneking, who told me, "We are in financial services, and all of us do exactly the same thing: we sell money. I thought, 'What if we changed this? What if we honestly, practically, demonstrably became advisors to the small businesses we serve?"

Now when the lender works with their small business cus-tomers, they are on the lookout for the elements they know make for long-term business success. Does the business have a good accountant? A good lawyer? A good financial advisor?

Being ready to provide a strong referral list of these resources helps learning-as-they-go business owners to (a) be aware of what they need from an experienced outsider, and (b) get what they need without expending significant time and research effort. The lender makes no money from these referrals, but providing them is what a good advisor does. It's what a partner with skin in the game does.

Services like this set the lender apart. It differentiates them.

You know differentiation when you see it

Differentiation, like love, comes in many shapes and sizes. Ben and Jerry's ice cream differentiated with a clever combination of amazing ice-cream naming conventions, and an unusually strong commitment to philanthropy.

Some ice creams names were simply clever, of course, like Jamaican Me Crazy or Berry Berry Extraordinary.

But they took naming conventions to a new level and continue to connect to their customer base. After President Obama's victory in 2008, they renamed a flavor Yes Pecan, a play on his "Yes, We Can" slogan, then donated all proceeds from the sale of that flavor to the Common Cause Education Fund.

And for faux-conservative talk show host Stephen Colbert, they created a flavor called AmeriCone Dream. They used their appearance on Colbert's late-night show to introduce the flavor, but also to introduce their grassroots education and literacy project designed to equip children to realize the real American Dream.

Maybe it's your product or your service. Or packaging. It could be your message or your over-the-top guarantee. Whatever form it takes, the result is the same: it gives you a distinct place in the heart and mind of your customer; it delivers you from being confused with your competitors.

These eleven idea starters advocated by John Jantsch of Duct Tape Marketing demonstrate the variety of approaches to differentiation. There's no "one size fits all" way to go about this.

1. Your product? Create something useful or trendy, or extend a product and offer a valuable service to make it more useful.

2. Your service? Consider a way to package what you do differently, like the executive coach who first told clients they'd pay him only if their employee feedback said they'd improved. This coach's process wasn't different from others but his payment equation was.

3. Your market niche? Dominate the niche you've chosen; being first makes you different.

4. Your offer? Fly with Southwest and your first and second bags fly free. Other airlines scramble to add what feel like snippy little charges (I'm waiting for coin slots on the restroom doors!), Southwest's offer sets it apart.

5. Your problem solution? Show how your answer provides unique relief, or more trustworthy relief to a deeply felt customer need.

6. Your messaging? Do a better job than anyone else of getting your value proposition to customers, telling your story through the formats and the vehicles that your customers use most.

7. Your unique "habit"? In nine major metropolitan areas, CVS Pharmacy runs something they call the "Good Samaritan Van." In a program that's been around for 30 years, drivers of these vehicles, who are trained in emergency auto issues and are also EMT's, come to the aid of motorists with flat tires, dead batteries, and other issues, all free of charge. CVS isn't an auto-repair company, but "this program is part of our vision to improve the quality of people's lives," a company spokesperson explained.

8. Your guarantee? What do your competitors guarantee? Can you be dramatically different? Or powerfully different?

9. Your customer support function? At a hosting and cloud computer company, a customer support employee in a marathon tech call overheard the customer telling someone in

the background he was hungry. She put the customer on hold, and ordered a pizza to be delivered to the customer's home. Thirty minutes later when the doorbell rang, the customer support person could announce that a pizza deliverer waited outside. That's differentiation.

10. Your knowledge of the competition? What are they missing that you do well?

11. Your attitude? Harley-Davidson makes distinctive motorcycles; so do others. But Harley sells a very particular kind of cool that makes them different than the rest.

Why differentiation matters

Differentiation makes the choice to buy from you easier. But if customers don't see how you are different from your competitors, you can count on near-invisibility.

If you are interested in competing on other than just price, differentiation is critical. The Marketto blog reports that in Europe, Coke offers customers the chance to customize their own Coke bottles with their names. And they're experimenting with a Coke can that twists apart to two smaller cans so you can share your drink with a friend. Check any grocery shelf: there are cheaper soda options than Coke. But Coke knows because they aren't competing just on price, they'd better be different.

Also, it reduces the bargaining power of your customers. They have the money you want, so the power rests in their hands until you offer them something they want more than their money. As you differentiate your product or service, that power equation shifts.

Deceptive indicators of differentiation

I find companies and brands think they are different when they aren't, so I now listen carefully for what I call "deceptive indicators of differentiation."

1. They are still generating revenue.

2. They are currently in a leadership position in their niche.

3. They price themselves differently from others.

4. They are constantly introducing product line extensions or new products, whether different or not.

5. They have something unique, but not relevant.

A conversation about these "deceptive indicators" doesn't always result in a move to change. Perhaps the company simply doesn't understand why differentiation is necessary to compete. In that case, education is in order. Or, the disinterest may come from arrogance. They are sure they know their market better than customers do, ignoring the fact that customers are the market!

Or, there can simply be the lack of a market-driven, problem-solving culture.

The company may have quietly given up. Owners don't believe they can differentiate, and have slipped into a commodity mentality. No reason to put forth the effort to differentiate themselves; there's nothing unusual to work with.

Sometimes simple laziness is behind these reluctances to change. Creating differentiation is often hard work, and takes careful scrutiny of the marketplace and the consumer. But what lazy companies miss is this: avoiding the work has a price, too.

As Sergio Zyman said in his book *Renovate Before You Innovate*, "preference is a perishable commodity; you must constantly refresh consumers' minds about the things that make you unique, why those things are important, and why they should buy your brand over someone else's. Not doing so can be expensive."

The powerful indicators

However, there are genuine indicators that point to the need to refresh, or strengthen differentiation. These five questions provide a high-level, but useful diagnostic for authentic differentiation. You want to know:

1. Is customer satisfaction eroding?

2. Are new products or programs failing or behind on expectations?

3. Are there disruptive innovations on the horizon?

4. Is there new competition?

5. Has an industry-wide communications audit revealed that everyone in your space is saying the same thing?

If any of your answers are affirmative, this may be the warning signal that points to a need to refresh differentiation.

Getting different, staying different

So, you are convinced, but you don't know how to start, or restart to establish differentiation? Here are ways to jump in.

Start by mapping the current landscape, looking for the places and ways everyone looks the same. You won't define what's new until you can clearly define the current state. In what ways are the products or services in your category obviously identical? What is everyone offering? How do you package the offering? Distribute the offering? Advertise/market the offering?

Understand the commonalities; these will help point you toward your most powerful disruptions.

Then, listen more closely to your customers than you do to your own internal company sensibilities. A majority of your people may love your current packaging – and those who created it may feel a deep investment in it. But do your customers see something different? And something that attracts them to your version above your competitors?

The most powerful moves you can make to increase differentiation rest on these two keys: (a) involve your customers' voices in the process, and (b) don't let untested assumptions or "how the industry always does it" drive decisions.

And mitigate the fear of change by starting with smaller steps. Experiment and measure. Experiment and measure. Experiment and measure. A commitment to evolution rather than revolution can still get you where you need to be if you keep moving.

It isn't enough to be good...

In the world your business inhabits, you have to be differently good to win. But the effort will pay off. I heartily endorse Theodore Levitt's view as he writes in Thinking About Management, "Differentiation is one of the most important strategic and tactical activities in which companies must engage."

Your investment in differentiating yourself will pay off.

34 · SUSAN SPAULDING

Leaders on Differentiation

Maria Meyers, Founder and Director, U.S. SourceLink & KC SourceLink

Some people fail to realize they have competition. If there's no visible competition, you can bet someone is behind the scenes, not yet visible, working on the same idea your company is championing.

Keith Pigues, Executive, Professor, Author and Speaker

There has to be more value than competitors. In this post recessionary era, companies are looking for innovation and growth. There has to be an understanding of how the company will deliver on economic value. You will always find the customer will place emphasis on different aspects than you were considering. A recalibration for differentiation has to employ the right tools to validate the opportunity and measure success.

Gary and Trish Walker, Co-Owners Magic Touch Cleaning, Inc.

We were the first janitorial company to go green in the Midwest. And we didn't give our customers the option to go green or not.

We weren't going to let our service people use toxic chemicals at one place, then be green at the next place. Introducing this concept was exhausting. It took all kinds of explaining what it meant and the rationale behind it. But the distinctive place it gave us in the marketplace paid off.

John Wendler, SVP Marketing, Tractor Supply Co.

Continual differentiation requires a growth mentality and a growth culture. Our CEO would say we are "relentlessly dissatisfied." We look at what we are currently doing, and then look for ways to break it – with improvement in mind.

So, our annual strategic planning process is something we are religious about. We talk constantly about Big Hairy Audacious Goals, not as a buzzword, but as a daily part of how we do business. We establish BHAGs company-wide, but stores set their own, too. And we love COEs – Collections of Errors. A COE review happens after every major initiative. How else will we learn what's working and what isn't?

Fred Embry, Power Group Companies

While building Embry and Company, a risk management firm, I worked hard to define my best customer, and I knew that customer to a "t". I looked for mid-tier (10-1000 employees), privately owned companies – but not necessarily in any specific industry. I knew this would work for me because larger companies have internal, dedicated risk managers.

Differentiating my business by company size and structure led to success.

Sandy Smith, AVP Opportunity Marketing, AmSurg

The ironic aspect of marketing Surgery Centers is the belief that patients choose surgeons rather than surgery centers. We have to be clear in our story and that hasn't been the case historically. You have to be ready for re-invention which doesn't mean you rethink everything every day but if we are not looking for opportunities everyday we are not going to find change and we won't be doing our job of building market share. We cannot be afraid to start something new. You have to try it out and see if it works.

CHAPTER FIVE

RECALIBRATING FOR

DIFFERENTIATION

BILL BERNARDO

APC CONSUMER PRODUCTS DIVISION

APC has been improving the lives of animals worldwide since 1981, when scientists identified the powerful role functional proteins play in helping support and maintain normal immune function in piglets. The company was first to initiate research on the benefit of plasma derived functional proteins for animal health and nutrition. Since then, APC has grown into the world's largest producer of functional proteins. Today they are a leading manufacturer of high-quality feed ingredients and complete, ready-to-serve products for the dairy, beef and equine industries.

When Bill Bernardo came on board to lead APC Consumer Products Division, the opportunity for disruption became quickly apparent. The market was what Bernardo described as a "sea of sameness." Everything looked the same, identical in packaging, colors and structure. So the time seemed right to turn things upside down, to differentiate.

Differentiating the promise

LIFELINE® is APC's leading brand in the animal health and nutrition category. To be trusted, Bernardo knew they had to communicate a promise that made sense, was authentic and highly relevant to the people they were specifically designing for. "We were not talking to everybody," he said, "our focus was on the thought and opinion leaders and those that move markets forward."

Many companies in Bernardo's space saw animal products as a side business, a place to push raw materials they couldn't use on the human side. So, brand promises didn't mean as much, and differentiation was typically lacking or nonexistent. It cost too much and was too much work.

Bernardo decided to position LIFELINE differently.

Working with a design firm, a compelling (and very authentic) tagline emerged: LIFELINE...Watch them Thrive. And that's the APC promise...LIFELINE helps your animal thrive.

To make this promise real, the team had to balance their own enthusiasm for delivery with expectations and stay true to strategy, focus, and capabilities. Otherwise the promise held no weight and delivery on the promise would be difficult, if not impossible. Product design and innovation played a huge role too.

Differentiating the customers

Users of the products turned out to be different from each other – by the type of animal owned – in how they shopped and bought. Farmers tended to be very pragmatic; they liked to buy in retail stores. Horse owners, on the other hand, wanted to buy their supplements online. Knowing not just what people wanted, but differentiating by getting those products into the right point-of-purchase settings made APC's offering unique and more valued.

Differentiating the connection to distributors

Retail buyers told Bernardo, "You are not like the average company we work with; you've got different thinking and innovation we haven't seen before. And, you understand our consumer better. "

Distinctive packaging first got their attention. Then, the rigorous and unique information the company provided made APC an easier choice for consumers. Effective marketing helped tell the story well, and complemented the eye-catching packaging.

Bernardo explained, "We spent a lot of time and money on understanding the market and identifying the right opportunities. As a result, the information we provided was very valuable to retailers because it helped them connect with their customers. And since we did the homework, we knew we could optimize the marketing mix better."

Differentiating internal communications

If insiders don't know what's going on, the best work won't get done. So Bernardo decided to create a philosophy known as "Collaborate & Communicate." This included quarterly stakeholder meetings (held offsite if possible) as well as weekly and monthly cross-functional team gatherings called "progress meetings."

Instead of solving problems, team participants reported project progress and determined what needed to happen next to keep the momentum going. The right people met in the right place at the right time and made sure the talk was actionable. From these meetings, priorities become clearer, so daily communications had a better chance to impact what mattered most.

"We also worked on creating visual symbols and icons and ways of structuring ideas that make them easier to understand and remember," Bernardo said. It was a way to address differences in communication styles; it also helped to overcome language barriers, important in APC's global operations.

Differentiation is usually spelled d-i-s-r-u-p-t

Bernardo describes the process of developing uniqueness this way: "You have to have a willingness to blow everything up and start over; it has to be your attitude going in, this willingness to look at it all differently and with fresh eyes. Once you're willing to adopt that mindset, new options almost always emerge."

Your offering becomes unique, and stays unique
when you keep pushing to differentiate
both internal processes and external promises.

CHAPTER SIX

ENGAGEMENT:

CONNECTIONS THAT

MATTER

Creating brand ambassadors of employees, consumers and
all those in the value chain by including them
in creating and delivering on what you do

The time, 1519. The place, Mexico, on the shores of the
Yucatan Peninsula. The characters, Spanish Conquistador
Hernando Cortez and his 600 men. The intention, to capture
the treasures of the Aztecs, an empire that had ruled the land
for over six centuries.

The odds were not in Cortez's favor, either in manpower
or might. But, as legend has it, he prevailed because he knew
how to generate engagement.

As his men faced battle against the Aztecs, quaking in their Spanish boots on this Mexican shore, he ordered, "Burn the ships! If we are going home, we are going on their ships."

Cortez gave his people no way out, only the challenge to find a way through. Lack of commitment wasn't an option; it was succeed or die. And, they succeeded against incredible odds.

Now, some report this tale as historically accurate; others call it urban legend. Either way, there's a principle with power here. Exactly what you do to emotionally engage your people and your customers with your brand is less important than that you are intentional about engaging them.

What is engagement?

Relevance in your strategy means you've defined what matters.

Differentiation means you've created a uniqueness that matters.

Engagement is the emotional "click" that happens when a connection that matters is made, between your proposition and your employees, and your proposition and your customers.

It's about building such an emotional, committed relationship with your people they become advocates, your unofficial sales force, your most loyal fans. When they are engaged, employees do more than required to move the company ahead, and they recruit their friends and family to work for you. When customers are engaged, they choose you first, prefer you, and insist on you. And they enthuse enough about you that others follow their lead.

Engaging at Apple

Engagement is the tenet in play when two strangers in an airport terminal waiting area huddle together over an iPhone while one shares with the other how to use the travel app that just allowed her to change flights while still in the waiting area.

Note that no one in this scenario is getting money from Apple to (a) sell the product, and (b) provide instruction in its use. But business traveler #1 is engaged enough, emotionally committed enough, to Apple's useful app that she wants to give away the time and energy required to tout it and teach it.

The same engagement shows up with Apple employees. As David Segal reported in *The New York Times* on June 23, 2012, at that time Apple stores were taking in more money per square foot than any other United States retailer, almost double that of Tiffany's, No. 2 on the list. Apple employees made the product successful, even though these tens of thousands of twenty-year-olds often earned as little as $25,000 a year.

However, financial gain looks different to different people. Apple's employees were hourly, but the company offered health care, 401(k) contributions and the chance to buy company stock, plus Apple products, at a discount.

Some would say these benefits helped protect Apple from disengaged employees, but the real story of engagement has to do with offering a higher purpose.

Apple hired those who loved the products and brand, and then offered them the opportunity not just to sell technology, but, as Apple described it, "to enrich people's lives." One manager reported it was common for people offered jobs to burst into tears. And new employee training was designed to turn employees into disciples. One said, "You've always been an evangelist for Apple and now you can get paid for it."

That's engagement.

And when it's not there...

You see disengagement. And now, increasingly, you hear it because it's online.

In a review called "The Worst Companies to Work for in 2013," msn.com named Radio Shack, the struggling consumer electronics retailer, who a year ago brought on its fourth chief executive in three years to try to create a turn-around.

His task is made no easier by employee comments culled from Glassdoor, an employer-review site. One employee wrote, "RadioShack constantly changes their focus because they are a struggling company. You'll be fighting real hard for one sales aspect and get told a month later that it doesn't matter anymore and that everyone is a failure." An assistant manager noted that a push to sell mobile phones resulted in having to foist services onto customers that realistically would not benefit them. Others complained about managers playing favorites among associates and store managers, and still others about district and regional sales managers imposing sales quotas that seemed arbitrary.

Disengaged employees have a voice that will increasingly impact your customers' perceptions of who you are and what you offer them.

Disengagement has a numbers-based face, too.

When I ask questions about disengagement, I look for these signs:

1. Is customer satisfaction declining?

2. Are customer complaints increasing?

3. Is employee satisfaction declining?

4. Is employee turnover increasing?

5. Is the company losing share to competitors?

6. Are channel partners reducing their buys?

Information about only one of these factors tells little about disengagement, but an aggregation of answers can point to significant issues.

If you want to more actively spread the word about your brand and products in ways that attract customers, and increase profitability with your current customers, you need engagement.

Ramping up engagement

With employees, involvement increases engagement. So when my clients increase collaborative problem-solving, or collaborative idea-creation, or collaborative strategy development (note the description for each item – yes, it's "collaborative") I know they are on the right track.

Sometimes greater involvement comes from simply knowing more about what's going on, what decisions are being made, what's ahead for the company. Some companies are aggressive about an internal intranet, or face-to-face town halls to be sure employees are the first to know, and know the most. Others use "internal champions" who function is not just carrying messages out to employees, but taking feedback in to help create dialogue when the sheer volume of employees makes dialogue difficult. When employees understand you care enough to let them inside, qualities like loyalty and brand evangelism have more chance to take root.

The same is true for customers. When they understand you care about what matters to them, engagement increases.

Care about them, they'll care about you.

Do your sales messages have more to do with you and the products you love than with what the customer needs and what the customer loves? Do you find yourself talking about your business by saying, "We produce [this product]"? Or do you say, "Our customers buy us to provide [this benefit]. We do that with..."

Your answer is more than just rhetorical tweaking. Increased customer engagement doesn't come just from little give-aways or snazzier YouTube contests. You'll increase engagement by being experienced as a catalyst to help the customer achieve her goals or meet her needs.

The CEO of Zappos.com says that, "every call is perceived as a way to make a positive emotional connection to the customer." It's this capture of minds and hearts – not just what we think, but how we feel about a company – that will influence buying decisions. It's the very essence of engagement.

Engagement starts with listening

When their customers' lives became busier, Walgreens originated the drive-through pharmacy and began refilling prescriptions at any location. When customers with English as a second language complained they couldn't read their prescriptions, Walgreens began printing prescription labels in 14 languages. And when older customers pointed out the labels were hard to read, large-type labels were introduced. Engagement-increasing innovations came from listening.

Listening to your employees works the same way. Harry Campbell is currently CEO of Durrie Vision. However, when he was president of the Consumer Markets Division of a Fortune 300 telecom, his 3,000-employee workforce included a significant number of retail employees, so Harry spent time in the stores, watching and listening. He wasn't there to check up, or to rank people; he was there to experience what it was like to be them.

One lesson came the hard way. The retail stores had tile floors, so after 2-3 hours of standing up working with customers, Campbell's back began to hurt. And had he actually been a sales associate there, he realized there'd be 5-6 more hours of this ahead. As he casually queried employees about this, he learned the problem was common, and they'd asked for chairs, but it was deemed unprofessional, and the request refused.

But this time a new solution was sought. Someone suggested high bar stools in the stores. This way, employees could sit or lean on them, but wouldn't be behind a table or counter, so accessible and welcoming. That little win, an occasional chance to rest, was a huge win on the engagement front. "You would have thought we had doubled their pay," Campbell reported.

But the solution didn't come from a "best practices" manual. Campbell looked at work through employees' eyes. That's what the best listening is about. It will make a difference in your workforce, and in your success with customers, too.

Engagement requires involvement

Engagement looks like a noun, but I consider it closer to a conjunction – "a part of speech that connects or joins together..."

Actions like engaging teams in decision-making, or showing them vulnerability by letting them know you don't have all the answers – these drive engagement. Or, like Harry Campbell, being as attentive to their needs as you expect them to be your company's interests.

Engagement pays

Engagement will pay in motivated, productive employees who are brand ambassadors.

But it will also pay off with sales. Ipsos MORI, a leading UK-based market research company, reported emotionally engaged customers are:

- At least three times more likely to recommend you
- Three times more likely to purchase again from you
- Less likely to shop around
- Much less price sensitive.

Aren't these the customers you're seeking? Maybe finding them will start by growing them – through involvement that leads to engagement.

Leaders on Engagement

Gary and Trish Walker, Co-owners, Magic Touch Cleaning, Inc.

Reprogramming the thinking of both customers and cleaners takes constant attention. We constantly have to remind them this is why we do things the way we do. But we know they've got it when we hear from them they've changed their own cleaning habits at home.

Claire Brand, VP and Innovation Platform Leader, Hallmark Cards, Inc.

We invited everyone in the company to be part of the innovation experience. We thought, why couldn't merchandising be innovative? Why can't packaging be innovative? Why can't these people innovate with us? We used to work through a more siloed process; you don't get the same quality in your results if everyone isn't in the same conversation from the beginning.

Gina Danner, CEO NextPage

I like having people around me with divergent thoughts. The worst thing a business owner can do is have people follow them aimlessly, who say, "What a great idea," to everything. I want my people saying, "That's kind of a good idea, but if we did this, that or the other, this could happen..." A red flag is waving to me if everyone thinks all my ideas are great all the time.

Gordon Harton, GFH Business Consulting, Inc.

Everyone in your organization needs to know the strategy. Everyone. And all need clarity about the actions their function group needs to take to make the strategy work. The things I believed were important, I asked about daily. If I called every week and asked the same questions, they got clear on what answers mattered to our success.

Mary Bentley, Marketing Executive, Food Industry

You have to have your own team in alignment - if they aren't, redirection is in order, and essential. Otherwise, each is left to clear all the hurdles alone. Working together means we are more likely to find different solutions that we'd have thought of on our own – and I think they are most often better solutions.

Dr. Michelle Robin, Your Wellness Connection, P.A.

One element I feel strongly about: if you come on board, you have to drink the Kool-aid. The passion can be there in many different ways but that interest, the curiosity, the involvement, that's what drives success and is the element that allows us to powerfully touch lives.

CHAPTER SEVEN

RECALIBRATING FOR

ENGAGEMENT

RICH MATHEWS

TOOLS BUSINESS DIVISION, NEWELL RUBBERMAID

Newell Rubbermaid Inc., an S&P 500 company, is a global marketer of consumer and commercial products with a strong portfolio of leading brands, including Rubbermaid®, Sharpie®, Graco®, Calphalon®, Irwin®, LENOX®, Levolor®, Paper Mate®, Dymo®, Waterman®, Parker®, Goody®, Rubbermaid Commercial Products® and Aprica®.

LENOX (unrelated to Lennox, a well-known brand of HVAC systems) is a 100-year old company that began by making hacksaw blades and is now a 900-person strong division of Newell Rubbermaid, manufacturing power tool accessories, hand tools and band saw blades.

With the acquisition by Newell Rubbermaid in 2003, LENOX moved quickly to recalibrate legacy brands and sell off products that had been acquired but didn't fit the division's core competencies. Paring back to the core led to focus, and new space for opportunities.

Rich Mathews said, "We had wonderful raw material to work with but there were far too many efforts going on. We had to answer the simple question: what are we going to stop doing so we can focus on the big things? How do we expand the portfolio in a way that makes sense?"

Looking for engagement

The company's core rested in their leadership position in linear edge cutting, but ever-improving competition was threatening that status. Communications focused on product features with little emotional content, even though differentiation to users was sliding.

The need was clear: to carry out a strong, clear compelling differentiated brand position that went beyond product features.

While a refreshed positioning was being pursued, new market opportunities were also sought.

Research pointed to the possibilities in the plumbing, electrical and heating/ventilation/air conditioning/refrigeration (HVAC/R) industries, but HVAC/R quickly rose to the top. An underserved customer base needed better tools; LENOX was well positioned to provide them.

Customers engage with products they help design

To get hold of the day-to-day lives of HVAC/R techni-cians, LENOX sent their people on more than 80 ride-along with HVAC/R techs. All together they visited more than 445 job sites; climbing ladders with the techs, baking in the sun with them on job sites, and climbing into small attics and dirty crawl spaces with them.

From these experiences it was clear that to their customers, HVAC/R techs were heroes. They came in when air condi-tioning was broken and it was 100 degrees outside. They showed up promptly, fixed the problem and got life and busi-ness back on track. So, HVAC/R techs had an emotional connection with their tools. Besides being easer to use and more efficient – thus making the techs' work easier – they needed to be tools the techs were proud to carry.

Then, meetings with 36 distributors followed by deep con-versations with the HVAC/R techs involving some 330+ people deepened and expanded these insights. In the process more than 60 product concepts were tested.

Market research honed the engagement strategy

Competitive market research showed the category had well-recognized brands, but they weren't really differentiated in the minds of consumers. Also, the techs didn't show a strong understanding how the tools could be better.

Because the LENOX brand generally carried clout in the world of tools, initial direction pointed to introducing LE-NOX-branded HVAC/R tools. But choosing to look at data rather than assumption led to a different conclusion. Research revealed confusion over the LENOX and Lennox brand names – two similar names in the same category. That information helped lead to the creation of another brand, hilmor.

During one planning meeting, a design engineer proposed dropping features because of the cost point. One product manager asked, "Why don't we find out what features people are willing to pay for before we start dropping them?" Subsequent research revealed the features in question could actually drive sales at higher price points, so were worth keeping.

When engagement starts early, it pays

LENOX suspected success lay ahead when the techs they'd invited to be part of focus groups tried the products, and responded they made 'total sense,' then asked after the groups ended, "Can I buy this now?"

Attention to the techs' way of working paid off when it came time to design advertising, too. A very clever ad campaign showcased one perfect tool against a classy, rich-looking dark green and black background, more like a setting suggesting a Lexus than a Kia. But the text that accompanied it played to the techs' insider wit.

In my favorite ad, something called a Compact Swage Tool that allows highly technical work in small spaces was featured center stage in a glossy, spotlighted photo. The words YOUR JEWELS were written under it in large letters. And clearly it looked like a jewel of a tool.

The subtitle read, "Thoughtfully designed to eliminate swinging a hammer at...YOUR JEWELS." Then in smaller print the ad explained, *In tight spaces you need a tool that can pack a punch. Just not below the belt. The all-new hilmor Compact Swage Tool can knock out a picture perfect swage in one shot. No sweat. No strain. No risk.*

One observer wrote that the marketing campaign, "playfully addresses current user frustrations..." Not trashy, not crass, but definitely clever. Since customers were predominately 18-49 year-old males, these ads created a story that engaged on both a humorous and visceral level.

Mathews said, "Launching a new brand is not for the faint of heart. We had lots of nights waking up in a cold sweat. But because we did the homework, we got most of it right."

Engagement creates a connection,
and the earlier it can begin,
the greater your chance of success.

CHAPTER FOUR

EXPRESSION: STORIES

THAT MATTER

Finding and delivering the essence of a

clear and compelling story to maintain engagement

with your target customers

You've perhaps heard the story. Even if you haven't, if you are female and living in America, you know the product. Spanx are undergarments that smooth out contours of a woman's body, making clothes more flattering and comfortable.

A great idea, but when product creator Sara Blakely tried to interest customers, they couldn't picture what she was describing.

So, when she managed to land a meeting with a buyer at Neiman Marcus, she showed up in a now-famous pair of form-fitting white pants, then surprised the buyer by inviting her to join her in the ladies room. Blakely proceeded to demonstrate what the pants looked like on her both with and without an assist from Spanx. The product was on Neiman Marcus shelves in three weeks.

Blakely said, "I wore those white pants for three years to sell Spanx."

A great founder's story, combined in this case with a wonderful tag line ("We've got your butt covered") can take a product from unmentionable to memorable.

A story tells and a story sells

The "our multi-billion-dollar company started in a garage" story has become so ubiquitous that in 2013, Cadillac created an ad for its CTS sedan featuring the garages in which the Wright Brothers, Amazon, Hewlett Packard, and Mattel started.

The founded-in-a-garage story has legs so long it has now even spawned a rebuttal in the form of Chip Heath's latest marketing book, The Myth of the Garage.

Dell computers took a similar advertising tack, linking their founder's story of a start-up in a dorm room with the "little room above the pizza place" where Travel Advisor was created, and the "dusty basement" where UnderArmour began. The successful Silpada jewelry company had a similar beginning.

All the stories you can tell

John Jantsch of Duct Tape Marketing defines four kinds of stories that matter.

The first is your founder's story of why the business started, what Jantsch calls a Passion Story. However, this is only one kind of Expression, a larger concept that must be part of your recalibrated market strategy. There may also be a Purpose Story of why you do what you do in business, along with a Value Proposition Story, describing what your brand delivers. A Personality Story lets people know how you want them to experience your purpose or brand.

All four kinds of stories have the same purposes. They answer all or part of three basic questions:

1. Why do your company and your product matter right now?
2. How is your problem solution different?
3. In what way will your solution make life better for your customers?

Expression is critical to a successful marketing strategy. Here's why: attention to Relevance will assure that what you do matches tightly with customers' needs. Differentiation defines your uniqueness, and Engagement will create emotional connections between your offerings and your employees and customers.

However, You may be relevant and unique, and able to generate emotion, but without the great stories that make up Expression, who will know?

When you get your story straight, you'll get your story told.

A straight story needs to be true

Back in 2010, an NBA franchise, the Minnesota Timberwolves, pushed the limits of truth-in-advertising in a most refreshing way.

For the previous five years, their record had been less-than-stellar, to put it kindly. They had, in fact, won a playoff series only one time in their 21 years of existence. But instead of asking fans to believe 2010 could be the turn-around year, they started with a straightforward look at reality.

Arrivals at the Twin Cities airport found a sign with the fierce-looking Timberwolves mascot, and this message:

We are not rebuilding.
We're re-re-re-re-re-re-rebuilding.
An honest assessment of the past.
A plan for the future.

Doesn't that do more for you than yet another chest-beating "we're-the-best" campaign? Your story can be true, and still be positive.

A straight story needs to be consistent

Detroit-based Quicken Loans almost over-communicates each step of the way so customers' experience in applying for a home loan is, well…quickened.

If your company story is centered on quickness, you'd better be sure the customers' experience is quick. Consistent stories are more believable stories.

A straight story has to be sold internally before it will sell externally

If I surveyed your leadership team individually, and asked where your company came from, what you care about, and why you do what you do, and how customers benefit from what you do, would all the answers be the same?

What about your employees? Could they tell me how their piece of the work process fits into the story? More pointedly, would they say their experience as part of your company aligns with the story, or disputes it?

What about distributors? And customers? How do they describe your promise to them? What parts of their experiences with you fulfill the promise?

Steve Jobs recounted, "Originally, we weren't exactly sure how to market the iTouch. Was it an iPhone without the phone? Was it a pocket computer? The customers told us they were seeing it as a game machine. We started to market it that way, and it just took off."

The deal breaker: ignoring employees

Everyone from your newest employees to seasoned leaders need to both know your story, and be living out a work experience that supports it.

Gina Danner, CEO of the print company NextPage, applied this principle when her company launched a newly-defined brand.

"We started with the team," she told me, "by throwing a brand launch party. But instead of introducing a bunch of visuals, we talked about what a brand was, and how the team and their individual interactions make or break a brand."

"We started with McDonalds, because everyone knew it so well. What do they get at McDonalds? High speed, low price. And at Applebee's? Speed, price? Yes, but not to the degree they'll find at McDonalds, and they know that going in, and expect more variety, a little better food, a beer..."

"Then I switched it up. The Capitol Grille is a well-known, high-end restaurant in our area, so I said, 'You can get a burger at McDonald's or Applebee's. And you can get a burger at Capitol Grille. Why would you go there for a burger when you know you are going to pay more for it and it will come to you more slowly than McDonald's?'"

Chewing on this question brought the team around to the heart of what telling a consistent brand story means. They'd pay more to go to Capitol Grille, we concluded, because the place and the people deliver more.

"Then I brought it back to us," Danner went on. "People can get business cards for free online. Why would people ever come to us for business cards?"

Her team got the point. What would distinguish their company wasn't going to be their print products alone. It was the capacity to deliver more than just print, and they'd need to deliver to that higher standard over and over.

"We want to be the Capitol Grille of print," they told me. "About then I pulled out a bag with the names of all 95 team members in it and drew out three of them, who then accompanied me to dinner at the Capital Grille."

The opposite of dinner out

CEO Ron Johnson's 17-month-stint leading JC Penney into a save-the-company turnaround was a dismal failure, and ended with his termination in 2013. This retail marketing genius who created the magic of the Apple Stores designed the most profitable retail operation in the consumer electronic industry. So, what happened?

The answer is partly about his lack of attention to Expression – to the crafting and testing and telling of a new story for JC Penney.

At Apple, Johnson started from scratch to create a customer experience and to choose the employees who would deliver it. But JC Penney already had a deep story as the retailer for low prices and ready bargains. And, they'd built a slow, steady, traditional culture based on this promise.

Steve Rosa at the Business Insider observed Johnson's defeat came largely because he moved ahead without being sure employees knew and believed the new story. There was little consumer testing for the company's new message of freshness and coolness; "no time to test," he said.

Rosa concluded, "Johnson tried to spark a retail revolution without a battle-ready army behind him. Like any army, his troops needed a cause to believe in, a code to follow, effective weapons and thorough training to have the best chance at victory."

Contrast this with Gina Danner's approach to re-branding at her printing company. The first participants in the story had to be employees. Once they became believers, they could help to both craft and deliver on the story to customers. Alignment.

When the story is fuzzy: commit to clarity

In my years of working with companies and their strategies, I find resistance to attending to story for one of these reasons:

1. They believe their products will sell themselves without the need to build the trust that great stories create.
2. They believe story telling is just an advertising function, rather than creating and delivering on a promise.
3. They don't know how to tell their story.
4. They don't know what the story is.

But I believe these companies are missing a rich and compelling experience of their brand through stories that are heard and felt. In time, they will miss the opportunity to build value. Expression creates not just awareness, but more importantly, customers who like, trust and respect you.

When the story is fuzzy: ask for help in clarifying

If your story needs a refocus, maybe you need to ask others what it is.

Seek out your employees; ask your customers; look for what others are saying about the products and experience you offer. In these connections I believe you'll recalibrate your story both accurately and effectively.

Leaders on Expression

Fred Embry, Power Group Companies

I believe it can be distracting from my ability to sell if I focus too much on selling my product or myself. I'm more interested in understanding my client's business and being sure what I'm introducing fits. I think I can show clients what my strengths are, but I'm more interested in understanding their strengths, their business, their vision, where they're going, what culture they want to create, what they're trying to accomplish. I'm more interested in helping them write their story than I am in telling mine.

Sam Meers, CEO Meers Advertising, Inc.

The story we're out to write with our clients is this: love something. Because if clients don't love their products, brand, company, the people they work with, their agency, their distribution channel, we're going to have a hell of a time trying to help them be successful. Likewise, if the people who work here don't love the agency, or the people they work with, or the products they are working on, they won't be successful. It's the "love something" theme that activates our brand.

Jeffrey Byrne, Principal Jeffrey D. Byrne + Associates, Fundraising

We differentiate ourselves by telling stories of successes we've influenced, through key leaders who've had successful projects with us. We let the work we've done speak for us.

Joyce Hayhow, Publisher Kansas City Business Journal

We are in an industrial revolution. The newspaper business has been the same for hundreds of years; all of a sudden everything got very different. Our philosophy turned upside down and we became digital first. But fortunately we have a veteran staff that embraced the change.

I think they did because in addition to an investment with the success of this newspaper, they are invested in the audience we serve and the community we live in. We've made our community a better place, helped advertisers grow their businesses, and helped each other grow professionally, plus balance work and family. Together, we feel a mission for what we do.

CHAPTER NINE

RECALIBRATING FOR

EXPRESSION

PAM BERNEKING

ALTERRA BANK

Since opening in 2010, Alterra Bank has experienced dramatic year-over-year growth and expanded from 14 to 43 employees. In 2013, the bank added a full-service mortgage division and a private banking team to better serve the bank's growing customer base. These divisions complement the bank's well-established commercial banking reputation. Since 2012, Alterra Bank has been Kansas City's #1 SBA Lender. Serving as Alterra's prototype for future growth, a new branch is staffed by "universal bankers" who can deliver a private-banking customer experience without traditional teller lines or drive-through lanes.

Alterra Bank began in 2010 when a group of bankers raised capital to purchase a troubled bank as a platform for future growth. The original investment premise was based on explosive growth fueled by acquisitions, taking advantage of disruption in the banking industry following the financial crisis. But the story didn't unfold as planned.

About the time of the purchase, the regulatory environment changed, and a closer look at the purchase showed inherent problems investors hadn't counted on. CEO Pam Berneking said, "We bought a $100 million bank, and found that about $50 million of the balance sheet wasn't business we wanted." The team had to work its way out of problems, losing nearly three-quarters of a million dollars the first year. In the meantime, regulatory winds were shifting and the acquisition environment went away.

Finding the heart of the story

Instead, Alterra chose a model of organic growth – and decided to become the World's Greatest Bank.

How would "Greatness" be defined? First, the World's Greatest Bank must be profitable; otherwise it would never be sustainable. But it wouldn't necessarily be the world's biggest bank, or the most successful, or the most profitable.

Berneking and her team decided the bank's greatness would be measured by the quality of its interactions with employees, customers, investors, and the community. "We are trying to add value to every interaction we have with any constituent," Berneking explains. "There's a quality to every interaction in the way we conduct it that leaves whoever we've engaged with a sense of added value, of feeling better because besides the business getting done, there's been fairness, openness, and transparency. And their business is better because they do business with us."

Creating services to carry the message

"We have to invest in the success of our clients because we expect them to invest in our success by doing business with us," Berneking explains.

"For example, a while back we felt we were trying to provide answers to a client with less than complete information. When we talked internally about the reason, we agreed this client probably didn't understand his cash cycle well enough, really didn't get how money flowed in and out of his business. We could have given a superficial answer, and that would have been easier, and actually cheaper for us, but it wouldn't have served the client."

"We decided to press, to ask questions, to push his learning in hopes of creating an 'aha moment' in which he said, 'Oh, my gosh! If someone paid me in 75 days instead of 60, it's going to significantly change my borrowing need.'"

That's what it means to Alterra to be the world's greatest bank – that extra effort to see a client succeed is the heart of their story.

Employees as storytellers

Berneking saw herself as the Chief Culture Builder, the keeper of the vision. So she made a priority of aligning employees to the vision. That meant keeping an eye out for people who loved banking, and who felt genuine energy and enthusiasm for it.

"Without banks economies don't thrive, and when banking struggles so do communities, so we had to have people here who got the importance of what we were doing," she explained.

But she also knew this vision and passion has to be cultivated with information. So she worked hard on open-book management to minimize an environment built on secrets, other than the ones required to operate in a highly-regulated industry. And she started regular lunch-and-learns both to continue to share the vision, but also so she could hear from employees about their challenges and their needs for resources or help.

Clients as co-creators of the story

Alterra decided greatness would mean not being all things to all people. Instead the team focused on being spectacular in an advisory role to clients. "Our ideal client," Berneking says, "is someone who'd call us their bank, and think of us – genuinely – as their partner. When they need a referral or recommendation, they pick up the phone and call us as quickly as others call their attorney or accountant or financial advisor."

And it would involve continual learning. Now the company's training program requires employees to de-brief with clients after providing service. They ask, "What was your experience? How did we make things better for you? What do you need that we don't have?" The answers inform the team's decision-making from services to technology additions.

From story to experience

"One client told us recently we saved his business because of a key decision that we helped him make," Berneking said. "In the middle of a quagmire, our advice and our approach to the situation helped him work through to a good solution. Now we are an integral part of his business plan, and he'll never go anywhere else. That's the story we're out to tell; the kind of experience we're out to create."

When you find the heart of your story,
both employees and clients need to be courted
as story-creators, then storytellers.
From this alignment, a consistent and true expression
will move you forward.

CHAPTER TEN

RECALIBRATION AS A VERB

The temptation with a tool like Recalibration is thinking you're finished with it.

You can put it away, or hold it in reserve for only the biggest crises: when things aren't going well, or when you've hit a batch of new opportunities, but your resources to capitalize on them are limited. Or when a change in leadership generates new expectations. Or when you are ready for a hand-off, to pass on the company, or sell it.

But to be effective, Recalibration can't be a once-and-done proposition, a name for something that starts and finishes. It has to be a verb; it has to become a continuous action, a way of life in your business.

Recalibrate continually with customers

You know your target market. You have a dedicated sales team talking to customers every day; you have people who analyze sales and market trends.

So why should you continually consult the customer? You have it down, right? Maybe not.

In a recent survey of business executives, I asked what they considered to be their top marketing issues. The number one need they listed was to understand what their customer valued.

These executives clearly recognized that because they knew the market five years ago or even one year ago didn't mean that they know what the customer wants today. The world is moving fast, and savvy consumers have more options than ever before. They have new problems, ever-shifting needs.

Customers want to be heard, so all you really have to do is ask. The answers are there.

The starting point? Make sure that the customer is always at the center of conversation. A few simple questions you can ask your customer include:

- What attracted you to us?
- What prompted you to buy from us?
- What is one thing we do better than others?
- What is one thing we can improve?
- Do you refer us to others; if so what do you say?

Then, use what you learn to both attract new customers and increase business with the customers you already have. And be attentive for clues they're offering to new market opportunities, and ways to create new experiences that sets you apart in their minds.

Continually recalibrate your brand

People yearn to connect to something important, or a community around something important. If you aren't making a meaningful connection with your target audience, they will seek out a brand that is relevant to them and your brand will soon be in decline.

But when you deliver on what you promised time after time, you create a community that continues to grow in numbers and through a deep emotional connection with your brand.

It's not just about good customer service and serving basic needs; it's about creating a great customer experience that connects them with your brand. That's what will prompt customers to give you great reviews and refer you to more people who will love you, too.

To create an outstanding customer experience you need to keep in mind the entire consumer journey: pre-purchase, purchase and post-purchase.

First, during pre-purchase – the "get to know you" stage – you want to create and maintain an authentic brand-building trust.

Next, during purchase – the buy stage – you want to continue to differentiate your brand from others and exceed expectations.

In the post-purchase experience you can create advocates who will readily refer others to your brand. It is not over just because a purchase was made.

Oftentimes, you need to re-invent your brand so that it feels like a new business. If you don't have new news, you can't expect growth. Naturally, people expect new things. However, be careful not to fall into the trap that any shiny new object will do.

Keep recalibrating your direction

What different results are you looking to achieve in your business? Do you need to keep up with advances in technology? Find ways to stay ahead of competitors? Improve your process flows to gain efficiency and save time? Fill your product pipeline? Increase customer share of wallet? Whatever results you are striving to accomplish, change must be at the center. And change starts at the top.

Figure out what you're really good at. Stop doing things that help pay the bills but are not going to lead to great things because other people do them better.

In order to regain control and focus, identify your three top priorities.

Then, clearly state your objectives so anyone in your company can understand what you want to achieve and how it will impact the company's growth.

Bring your team together to generate ideas and develop a blueprint of how the objectives can be achieved. Let the team help identify the resources needed to get there and how it can happen with recalibrated priorities.

Then, communicate clearly the agreed-upon plan of action to meet the objectives. Having stretch goals and objectives helps you overachieve. Having illogical, outlandish goals sets you back.

Visualize exactly what your definition of success will look like and track your progress so you know when further recalibrating is needed. Choose some simple but illustrative devices to demonstrate progress.

If the organization is going in too many different directions, have the re-set start with you. Alignment on top priorities will build momentum as you work toward your goals. Reporting progress will help you recognize achievements and spur any necessary adjustment without derailment.

Recalibrate employees, again and again.

Out of all the resources within the organization, your people are the most valuable. Technology and processes have their place in the company; however, success starts with people and it grows with people.

The first time the employee walks through your door, brand indoctrination should begin so that the employee knows the story you wish to communicate. However, it is only a beginning. If you are not continuously repeating the story then people bail out too quickly.

So, how do you get a diverse group of employees to align on a common goal and message? The expression of your story and the conviction to deliver on brand promises are key. And, all those connecting points with employees matter too – lunch-and-learns, town halls, intranet posts, newsletters and e-mails.

Your investment in aligning employees will pay off; I guarantee it, because I've seen it happen time and again. You'll find aligned employees will improve the value of your company, gain credibility for you as provider of a great place to work, and generate a culture of innovation.

A small step toward recalibration may push you into the winner's circle

We've looked at ways to recalibrate your business from many directions; it may feel overwhelming. However, according to one of the liveliest leadership authors I know, Harry Campbell, you may not need to get everything recalibrated perfectly to win. In his book *Get-Real Leadership*, he explains it this way:

"There are 162 games in a baseball season. Every team in the major leagues is going to lose 40 and win 40 no matter how good they are and no matter how large or small the payroll they carry."

"However, there are 82 other games that each team plays. You know what happens in those other 82? While size of payroll may be a factor, history has proven that no matter whether you spend a lot or a little on players, the winning teams do the little things extremely well."

"They hit the cut-off man in the fifth inning, make the right pitching change at the right time, turn the double play in a crucial situation, block the ball in the dirt with a runner on third and they win frequently, often by one or two runs."

"They win 62 and lose only 20 of those other 82 games. In total, they win 102 games and go to the World Series."

"The cumulative effect of dozens of little, positive and productive choices, decisions, and plays enables them to tip the balance and win a majority of the games that are toss-ups. These teams find a way to win at the margin when the game is in the balance."

Recalibration will show you just where those margins are for you, and keep you on a path to winning for years to come.

ABOUT RECALIBRATE STRATEGIES

Recalibrate Strategies helps organizations develop strategies to accelerate business and brand growth. We facilitate a collaborative process that harnesses insights, generates ideas, and develops strategic blueprints for:

• Business Strategies: Clarifying Vision, Mission, Core Values, Goals, Strategic Imperatives, and Accountability
• Brand Strategies: Ensuring a brand is being expressed so that it is relevant, differentiated, and engaging at every touch point
• Marketing Strategies: Using a systematic approach to focus resources where there will be the greatest results
• Innovation Strategies: Introducing and/or recalibrating the innovation engine to be market driven and increase commercialization success

Ideal clients . . .

• wish to accelerate growth and profitability.
• have great passion for what they do and seek to evolve the business.
• have an avid interest in listening to the customer.
• are sincere in engaging teams in the vision of the business

Recalibrate Strategies offers leadership training designed to increase customer growth, brand growth and organizational success. It integrates the concept of recalibrating into the culture, helping organizations uncover new possibilities.

You will learn:

• How to harness the knowledge that already exists within your organization
• Ways to break down the barriers to change and introduce the premise of disruption and creative problem solving
• How each of Recalibrate's RDEE tenets apply to your business:
> 1. What is relevant
> 2. What is differentiating
> 3. How to engage your customer, your key influencers and your organization
> 4. How to tell your story
• What measurements matter
• What the red flags are and how to turn red flags to opportunities

For more information, visit us at recalibratestrategies.com.

ABOUT SUSAN SPAULDING

Susan Spaulding is the founder and leader of Recalibrate Strategies. The consulting firm leverages her experience as a business owner and strategist as well as her expertise in marketing, communications and insights to help organizations recalibrate their business and brands.

Susan brings an entrepreneurial mindset to her work, allowing her to see and communicate new possibilities that lead to great outcomes. Susan has a natural talent for quickly framing the toughest issues to make them newly accessible from multiple perspectives. She enables her clients—from start-ups to the Fortune 100—to focus on business and brand growth strategies.

Susan formed Market Directions as a subsidiary of one of the largest advertising agencies in Kansas City. After acquiring Market Directions, the focus of the firm evolved from a traditional market research firm to a brand performance consultancy that Susan owned and operated for many years. As a result of this positioning, Market Directions was acquired by a top 50 Honomichl market research firm, The Pert Group. Susan was a principal in that firm helping shape the organization to be a global market research consulting firm.

Now she is pursuing once again her love affair with entrepreneurship through Recalibrate Strategies, as a licensed marketing consultant for Duct Tape Marketing and the launch of Complete Growth International, an enterprise focused on providing a suite of measurements that matter to uncover where there is opportunity to recalibrate.

Her leadership in the industry is recognized locally, nationally and globally. She has served as Board Member for the Council of Survey Research Organizations, the Business Marketing Association, the American Marketing Association, and the Association for Corporate Growth as well as a variety of non-profit and advisory Boards. Further, she is recognized by the Kansas City Business Journal as a Women Who Mean Business honoree and by the Greater Kansas City Chamber of Commerce, which named her company Market Directions as a Top Ten Small Business in Kansas City.

Outside of her many hours at work, she spends time with family, good books, a glass of wine and in great conversation. With her husband, Susan logs numerous hours of cross-country driving in a 1967 Austin Healey 3000 and has enjoyed barnstorming in a Piper Cub.

Made in the USA
Charleston, SC
06 May 2014